~ The Parable Of ~
· The Broken Violin ·

· A Parable On Burnout and Brokenness ·

~ By: B.N. ~

BC. Neon Publishing

P.S. Doodle Something. Make it yours.

In a conversation with a good, long-standing friend, about how broken they felt after a difficult separation with a partner, they made an analogy about being a broken instrument.

Let me assure you, in the hands of a skilled enough craftsman, nothing is too broken to be made, remade, or incorporated into something much bigger, and far more beautiful. Even you.

Dial (998) for the U.S. Crisis Hotline

Last checked 2025

Thank you, *L.*, for showing everyone around you, that even when healing old wounds, we can still be everything we need ourselves to be.

Each Page will be left mostly blank for your convenience.

Perhaps you'll have your own inspirations to add.

Because…

Imagine, just for a moment...

You were a violin player.

But not just any violin player...

A *Prodigy*.

If for a moment, imagine...

Your life changed when you first touched the string of a violin...

But you were just a child.

How wonderful it was to play for the first time.

First it was fun.

Then you were given lessons.

And now, it was *proud*...

Oh, how you loved that violin.

You started off good, and now you were *great*.

Years of performance...

Years of practice...

You were one of the best...

In fact, even before you were all grown up...

You were invited to play in front of thousands of people...

The applause was deafening,

and the achievement was euphoric.

From the beginning to *right then...*

All on the same violin.

Life revolved around your violin.

You loved it, after all.

After all, you were *made* by the violin.

Every choice you made was to play.

To play with an audience...

To play for your loved ones...

To even play alone...

You loved it.

So you played...

In concert...

With the ones you love...

All by yourself...

Even with the ones who didn't love you…

or your violin…

And when your strings began to snap…

You made a choice to replace them.

And when your bow needed hair...

You cut off your own.

After all, you and your violin were one in the same.

SNAP ...

TEAR ...

CRASH ...

Somehow, someway, the violin shattered...

And you thought,

What am I supposed to do now?

After all, you and your violin were one in the same.

You lost your first seat...

All your solos…

All your praise.

The mirrors didn't seem the same…

And the space you occupied seemed so much...

smaller.

Instead of you on the pedestal...

Was your broken violin...

But I was you and you were me...

Dial (998) for the U.S. Crisis Hotline

Last checked 2025

And when you touched the pieces...

All you felt was your own skin.

KNOCK KNOCK KNOCK...

People came and people went...

Some with intentions, some with curiosity...

But none were there for you...

Turns out, you were not your violin...

And as it would seem,

Less important than it too...

May I?

Someone asked, taking the violin.

You know, I saw you in concert a few times.

You are amazing...

Can you teach my students to play?

What could you lose?

Take the chance...

So you began teaching...

And your students couldn’t see a string from a rope.

Day by day, they got better...

and better...

Because of *you.*

In front of their families...

In front of their schools...

And in front of the ones they love...

Because of *you*.

Time and time passed by.

And your students did not see a violin,

And instead, they saw you.

KNOCK KNOCK KNOCK...

I've been working on your violin...

I could never play like you...

but I was good with my hands...

It'll never sound the same...

but someone like me will

never hear the difference...

And he handed you your violin…

Somehow fixed...

Somehow new...

With scars exactly where it had broken...

Perfectly smoothed out...

And he was right,

it didn't sound the way it used to.

But for those who *always* saw you,

and saw you play the violin...

One, and one...

It was beautiful all the same...

And always was.

And always will be.

~ The Tears ~
· Of A Perfect World ·

· A Thought Experiment On Suffering ·

~ By: B.N. ~

After the passing of a very, very close friend of mine, a thought experiment that I had come up with had resurfaced in my mind as I was in grief. That even in a perfect world, suffering was inevitable. And in all the suffering I had witnessed, I knew it was better to be together than alone in it.

Thank you, *D.*, for your wonderful presence in all the lives you touched. Despite your wounds, you made this world a far better place than how you found it.

Imagine again…

A *perfect* world.

Where everyone made the *right* choice.

Always and *every* time.

It was *always* fair.

It was *always* charitable.

Always loving.

Always.

And once upon a star…

A long, *long* time ago...

The star died in a glorious supernova…

Long before your first ancestor...

And out came a *single* cosmic ray...

And one day, to *no one's* fault…

The cosmic ray passed through you...

Causing enough damage to make you very sick...

Would you want to be alone?

No one to comfort you...

No one to help you...

And no one to help?

Yes, suffering *can* be needless…

And yes, there are many dimensions to life

that bring us together.

But suffering is not useless.

To anyone's or no one's fault…

Suffering is one of many seeds...

That spawn comfort, growth,

and unity to our lives...

Togetherness...

Always.

Never Alone.

Dial (998) for the U.S. Crisis Hotline

Last checked 2025

~ Good Bye ~

<3

- In Memoriam -

Lola

Megan

Cameron

David

~ Thanks for being you till the very end

www.ingramcontent.com/pod-product-compliance
Lightning Source LLC
LaVergne TN
LVHW020047110826
845155LV00029B/675

* 9 7 8 1 9 5 4 3 8 9 1 4 4 *